furuike ya
kawazu tobikomu
mizu no oto

old pond ...
a frog leaps in
water's sound

Basho. tr. William J. Higginson

RAINSONG

2014 Seabeck
Haiku Getaway Anthology

Chandra Bales and Susan Constable, Editors

Haiku Northwest | Vandina Press

Haiku Northwest
Vandina Press

Copyright © 2015 by Haiku Northwest

All rights revert to the authors and artists upon publication in this book. No part of this book may be used or reproduced in any manner whatsoever without written permission from the contributor, except in the case of brief quotations in reviews.

This collection of poems commemorates Haiku Northwest's seventh annual Seabeck Haiku Getaway, held October 16–19, 2014 at the Seabeck Conference Center in Seabeck, Washington.

ISBN 978-1-887381-29-1

Layout and Design by Chandra Bales

Cover and Flyleaf Photographs by Carole MacRury
Haiga and Sumi-e by the Haiga Adventure Study Group of Puget Sound Sumi Artists

Poems and Prose set in Minion Pro
Titles and Headings set in Lucida Sans Unicode

Haiku Northwest | Vandina Press
Bellevue, Washington
www.haikunorthwest.org

Sound Haiku

rain notes wind riff frog grunt tree ease sshh

Sound Haiku: Written with sound as a topic
or as a poetic device—our theme
for the 2014 Seabeck Haiku Getaway

Michael Dylan Welch and Angela Terry put together a delightful, fully packed few days of presentations, forest bathing, book-making, readings, anonymous haiku, renku, and talent for the 2014 Seabeck Haiku Getaway. Activities began Thursday afternoon with check-in, socializing, and Margaret McGee's double spiral labyrinths. She and volunteers created them in a large grassy area with a fantastic view (which could be anywhere and everywhere at Seabeck!), using branches, leaves, shells, pinecones, and bones. We also made weathergrams, writing haiku on brown paper tags and tying them to tree branches or lacing them into the labyrinths.

That evening after dinner and more socializing we met at Coleman Center, and Michael welcomed us and led a round of haiku reading. Then John Stevenson organized us into a "haiku map," based on home states, provinces, and territories. We each spoke one word to represent an expectation for the weekend. Later, resident cartoonist Jessica Tremblay created a word cloud of our desires for passion, inspiration, friendship, and much more. You can see Jessica's wonderful Seabeck comics and photos at www.oldpondcomics.com.

After Michael explained the weekend's ongoing renkurama, our featured guest Alan Pizzarelli read from his book *Frozen Socks: New and Selected Haiku*. Susan Constable presented ideas for writing haiku with sound and played aural prompts. Throughout the weekend we were encouraged to start renku and to link to verses on the in-progress renku sheets. Those of us with stamina to *haiku* into Thursday night joined Kathy Munro for an anonymous haiku workshop and "burning questions" discussion. Deborah Kolodji led the workshop and discussion on Friday night.

Margaret guided us in inspiring and mindful-of-the-moment labyrinth meditations in the mornings, and then we enjoyed breakfasts in the dining room. In fact, we ate well all weekend, with plentiful dishes at each meal. At Coleman Center we heard and participated in thoughtfully prepared workshops, panel discussions, and readings. Alan gave a personal and thorough perspective on American haiku over the last fifty years and, with Donna Beaver, presented *Haiku Chronicles*, their journey into multimedia and podcasting. Visit their Web site at www.haikuchronicles.com.

Susan Callan led a lovely workshop where she taught us how to make a flag book, "an elegant haiku keeper." She put together an impressive array of decorative papers and offered friendly guidance as we each created a flag book. Some had filled their own book with haiku and artwork by the end of the Seabeck getaway.

Aubrie Cox reminded us in her presentation on haibun and musicality that haibun is a poem; read it aloud and pay attention to language and poetic devices. That awareness echoed in the later panel discussion on haiku as poetry, with thoughts, questions, and answers from Aubrie, Deborah, Alan, John, and Michael.

This Seabeck getaway was a bit wet, but rain did not deter our Friday night ginko, made solemn and beautiful with the blue glow of Japanese paper lanterns. And Angie further rewarded us with chocolates in the forest cathedral.

The Seabeck kukai is a getaway tradition. This year, each participant had two index cards, wrote an anonymous haiku on each card, and put them in the "haiku snake" (serpent?). Angie and Michael numbered the cards and placed them on a circle of chair seats; then we each wrote out our rankings for the haiku. All numbers were written on the board and we voted for our favorites. Poets with the top numbers of votes received prizes of notebooks and hand-crafted paper. Read the winning haiku and senryu in the "Kukai Winners" section.

Saturday evening Joey Clifton (a.k.a. Alan) hosted a "gala roast" of Michael Dylan Welch—a spirited and hilarious gathering! But before that we entertained and were entertained by each other at the Great Seabeck Talent Show and Music Jam. Barbara Hays introduced all of us to palm pipes. We each had a pipe, color-coded by length; we hit the end of the pipe on the palm, matching the pipe color to colors on the projected diagram—et voilà, music! Stories, cabaret-style haiku, singing, more music, and dancing: we were a rowdy and happy group. And, ready to roast!

We are a creative group in other ways, from our haiku sheets and books to our handmade name tags to the Puget Sound Sumi Artists' paintings and haiga. And we are generous, donating wonderful items for the silent auction to support Haiku Northwest and their Seabeck Haiku Getaway—and preparing and presenting talks, readings, and workshops. Here are more of the events we enjoyed.

"A Haiku Trip to Japan" — Michael Dylan Welch

"Should the First Be Last?" — Deborah Kolodji

"Gift of the Land: Yukon Seasons" — Kathy Munro

"Haikuilts" — RaNae Merrill

Haiku readings — Deborah Kolodji, Tanya McDonald, John Stevenson

"Editor: Gatekeeper and Mentor" — John Stevenson, in discussion with the group

"Celebrating Seabeck's 100th Anniversary" — Chuck Kraining

"Poems from the Shuswap: Haiku by Laryalee Fraser" — Carole MacRury, Susan Constable

"Haiku on Steroids" — Michael Dylan Welch

Porad Haiku Contest results — John Stevenson, flute music by James Rodriguez

"Nature Walk: Sounds and Other Senses" — Ruth Yarrow, recorded by Alan Pizzarelli and Donna Beaver

"400 Years of Sound in Japanese Haiku" — Richard Tice

Haiku readings — Aubrie Cox, Christopher Herold, Karma Tenzing Wangchuck

No Longer Strangers (Haiku Northwest's 25th anniversary anthology) reading — coordinated by Michelle Schaefer, flute music by James Rodriguez

Renkurama reading — Michael Dylan Welch, Angela Terry

"Old Pond Comics: Out of the Woods" —
   Jessica Tremblay

"Monkeys Invade the Sacred Palace and Chase Out
   the Tiger" — Alan Pizzarelli

And Terry Ann Carter presented a touching workshop on "Chiyo-ni and Aisatsu: Composing Greeting Haiku." Terry Ann gave us each a sheet of rice paper on which we wrote a greeting haiku to give to the friend at our side. Marco Fraticelli (Quebec, Canada) enhanced the pleasure of this *aisastsu* custom with the surprise gift of a booklet of selections from his in-progress work *Fragments: The love letters and haiku of Chiyo-ni.*

Please enjoy the haiku and senryu that we created in response to the Seabeck Haiku Getaway, the photographs from Carole MacRury, and the haiga and sumi-e from the Haiga Adventure Study Group of Puget Sound Sumi Artists.

— Chandra and Susan

beneath the rain
we share the warmth
of words

Haiku and Senryu	1
Kukai Winners	71
Poets and Places	83
Credits	91

Haiku and Senryu

driftwood
I shift my weight
with the ferry

Aubrie Cox

the geese call
on practice runs
drifting cloud

Carole Slesnick

crossing the old car bridge—
each board thrumming
a different pitch

Rick Clark

geese on the tide flats
honking at the moon
we arrive after hours

Ann Spiers

this floating world
under a line of umbrellas
paper lanterns

Richard Tice

Neptune and Uranus,
blue spheres in the sky—
night ginko

lynne j

new to me
by the light of a paper lantern
… an old friend

Carole MacRury

cra-ack cra-ack
frog breaks
morning silence

patty hardin

walking to breakfast
I hear tree tops grunt and groan
aahhh cormorants

Lynne Mustard

October morning
more urgent than yesterday
the flight of geese

scott galasso

empty rocking chair
the steady squeak
of a tree frog

Tanya McDonald

Halloween on the stoop tree frogs handing out croaks

Ann Spiers

falling leaves
the little girl rocks
all the rockers

jim rodriguez

featured speaker—
his name emblazoned
across his chest

Carole MacRury

new jersey man
his bromley hat
brushed with blossoms

Elaine Harvey

the applause
of turning pages
haiku speaker

Michelle Schaefer

the haiku meeting
goes on and on …
a steady rain

Johnny Baranski

sound of wind-rain
she opens
      the door

Chandra Bales

a rustle of leaves
in the autumn forest
when do you retire?

Rachel Eno

cedar branches
as silent as the moon
misty rain

Michael Dylan Welch

tree frogs
in the morning rain
flute echoes

Angela Terry

skipping stones
the sound
of her reflection

patty hardin

wooden bridge
arches over low tide—
our hollow footfalls

Ruth Yarrow

Far from the feeder
the hummingbird hovers
by my ear

Adrienne Drobnies

rain gurgle
his version of
Jabberwocky

    (for MDW)

    Terry Ann Carter

autumn rain
a crane fly enters
the belly dance

    Vicki McCullough

far-off ocean view
I close my eyes
to hear the sound

Michelle Schaefer

another ocean
same rhythm
of breaking waves

scott galasso

waves lap the shore
we sing a round
around the fire

RaNae Merrill

blues haiku
even the raindrops
riff

Terry Ann Carter

walking the labyrinth
my life unravels
silence

>*lynne j*

a raindrop
bounces off
a fallen apple

>*Jessica Tremblay*

autumnal labyrinth—
the twists and turns
of silent thoughts

Kathleen I. Tice

haiku gathering
cacophony of raindrops
and spoken words

Ruth Yarrow

dinner bell ignored
　　at the haiku reading ...
food for thought

Christopher Herold

bell street
the silent drone
blinks

Dianne Garcia

vespers bell
metal on metal pulsing
through the trees

Terran Campbell

the deer and I   silence

Vicki McCullough

apple grove
the black-tailed deer walks
toward us

Aubrie Cox

in the silence
an apple
falls

Elaine Harvey

rain on pines
to the west | to the east
rain on apple trees

Richard Tice

forest pattering—
the mushrooms too
have umbrellas

Rick Clark

night walk—
we all return
wet from the woods

Michael Dylan Welch

autumn deepens one last dandelion

John Stevenson

wind tugs my kite—
the gift
of letting go

after Chiyo-ni

Sue Mackenzie

raindrops
on salmonberry leaves …
a child's gravestone

Kathleen I. Tice

music swirling
from a wooden flute
what's lost what's found

Sheila Sondik

years
    since your passing
stair
   step
      moss

Deborah P Kolodji

passing clouds
the silence of those
no longer with us

Johnny Baranski

child tombstone—
a flower
is how you can tell

Jessica Tremblay

sunlight through the alders
deepen the shadows
of giant ferns

Alan Pizzarelli

mycology lesson
do I dare touch
witch's butter?

CR Manley

who who who
hidden in darkness
witness protection

Adrienne Drobnies

in the still silence
the slow fall
of cottonwood seeds

Alan Pizzarelli

wigeons whistling
in the wet grass—
this too-packed schedule

Tanya McDonald

the precise timing
for the next high tide
Seabeck dinner bell

Barbara Snow

talk of silence—
from deep in her bag
a ringing phone

Susan Constable

in the mime's hand
    how loud
   the fan

Barbara Snow

the deaf poet
writes about sounds—
one hand clapping

Sue Mackenzie

palm pipe
the last of the
travel-size shampoo

kjmunro

his breath
chanting the notes
flute player

Chandra Bales

talent show—
a crane fly floats
with the music

Angela Terry

the warmth
of Grandmama's quilt
autumn rain

Darlene McCourt

bedtime reading hai

RaNae Merrill

a midnight phone call
whiteness
of my breath

Rachel Eno

soft autumn rain—
a rowboat bumps the piling
on the lagoon

Barbara Hay

over the traffic
the chirping of one
determined sparrow

Terran Campbell

leafy labyrinth
its pathways rearranged
by the wind

Sheila Sondik

walking meditation
   first the twin labyrinth
      then the bouncing bridge

Christopher Herold

i watch my resolve
shaky as ever
crossing the bridge

Carole Slesnick

crackling across the porch
mottled leaves
from the big leaf maple

Ida Freilinger

patchwork of kids
in the museum—
half-eaten apple

Barbara Hay

museum ginko—
I stare at a doll
staring at me

Priscilla VanValkenburgh

autumn wind
two ladies strum
air guitar

Katharine Grubb Hawkinson

attracted
by tree frog mating songs
the poets

CR Manley

the circle of women
discussing 69
I wet my lips

jim rodriguez

snack wrapper crackles
peanut butter chocolate
no app for that

Lynne Mustard

licorice candy
the stickiness
of words

Dianne Garcia

scimitar moon
she wears her Dracula T-shirt
to the feedback session

Margaret D. McGee

evening calm
an open parenthesis
of moonlight

John Stevenson

flute notes ending the sound of rain

Susan Constable

night ginko
the silence of paper lanterns
carried in the dark

Priscilla VanValkenburgh

rainy night ginko—
white bulb lanterns
bob in single file

Ida Freilinger

moonlight sonata
the dance
of a crane fly

Deborah P Kolodji

crossing the border into Canada geese flying south

kjmunro

Kukai Winners

First Place

starless night
the puddle finds a hole
in my shoe

Susan Constable

Second Place

open window—
a frog contributes
his opinion

Barbara Hay

Third Place

woodland chapel ...
the slug cradled
in a brown leaf

Vicki McCullough

Fourth Place (Tie)

dimly lit
lecture after lunch
the laptop falls asleep

kjmunro

autumn rain …
walking from one labyrinth
into another

Richard Tice

forest walk—
the wind too
weaving through trees

Carole MacRury

Fifth Place

Japanese lanterns
the glow hushes
into single file

Michelle Schaefer

Sixth Place (Tie)

no beginning
no end
sound of water

Patty Hardin

children's graveyard—
pine needles holding on
to last night's rain

Carole MacRury

Seventh Place (Tie)

windless night
we listen to leaves
catching rain

Susan Constable

moss clinging
on a dead branch
he finally let her go

Carole Slesnick

labyrinth of leaves
with a single gust
thoughts blown away

Christopher Herold

cedar grove—
what a racket it's making,
that frog!

Karma Tenzing Wangchuk

Poets and Places

Chandra Bales [14, 48]
    Albuquerque, New Mexico

Johnny Baranski [14, 41]
    Vancouver, Washington

Terran Campbell [29, 56]
    Seattle, Washington

Terry Ann Carter [22, 25]
    Victoria, British Columbia

Rick Clark [5, 33]
    Seattle/Ocean Shores, Washington

Susan Constable [46, 65, 73, 79]
    Nanoose Bay, British Columbia

Aubrie Cox [3, 31]
    Taylorville, Illinois

Adrienne Drobnies [21, 43]
    Vancouver, British Columbia

Rachel Eno [15, 51]
    Burnaby, British Columbia

Ida Freilinger [58, 66]
    Bellevue, Washington

scott galasso [9, 24]
    Edmonds, Washington

Dianne Garcia [29, 63]
    Seattle, Washington

patty hardin [8, 20, 78]
    Long Beach, Washington

Elaine Harvey [13, 31]
    Victoria, British Columbia

Katharine Grubb Hawkinson [60]
    Seattle, Washington

Barbara Hay [55, 59, 74]
    Ponca City, Oklahoma

Christopher Herold [28, 57, 79]
    Port Townsend, Washington

lynne j (Lynne Jambor) [7, 26]
    Vancouver, British Columbia

Deborah P Kolodji [40, 66]
    Temple City, California

Sue Mackenzie [38, 47]
    Victoria, British Columbia

Carole MacRury [7, 12, 76, 78]
    Point Roberts, Washington

CR Manley [42, 60]
    Bellevue, Washington

Darlene McCourt [50]
    Everett, Washington

Vicki McCullough [22, 30, 75]
    Vancouver, British Columbia

Tanya McDonald [10, 45]
    Woodinville, Washington

Margaret D. McGee [63]
    Port Townsend, Washington

RaNae Merrill [25, 51]
    New York, New York

kjmunro (Kathy Munro) [48, 67, 76]
    Whitehorse, Yukon Territory

Lynne Mustard [8, 62]
    Victoria, British Columbia

Alan Pizzarelli [42, 44]
    Bloomfield, New Jersey

jim rodriguez [11, 61]
    Washougal, Washington

Michelle Schaefer [13, 23, 77]
    Bothell, Washington

Carole Slesnick [4, 58, 79]
    Bellingham, Washington

Barbara Snow [45, 47]
    Eugene, Oregon

Sheila Sondik [39, 57]
    Bellevue, Washington

Ann Spiers [5, 11]
    Vashon Island, Washington

John Stevenson [37, 64]
    Nassau, New York

Angela Terry [19, 49]
    Lake Forest Park, Washington

Kathleen I. Tice [27, 39]
    Kent, Washington

Richard Tice [6, 32, 76]
    Kent, Washington

Jessica Tremblay [26, 41]
    Burnaby, British Columbia

Priscilla VanValkenburgh [59, 65]
    Liberty, Utah

Karma Tenzing Wangchuk [79]
    Port Townsend, Washington

Michael Dylan Welch [15, 33]
    Sammamish, Washington

Ruth Yarrow [21, 28]
    Seattle, Washington

Credits

furuike ya/old pond   [flyleaf (i)]
The Haiku Handbook: How to Write, Teach, and Appreciate Haiku, 25th Anniversary Edition.
William J. Higginson and Penny Harter.
Kodansha America, 2009.
Reprinted with permission of Penny Harter.

Photographs: Carole MacRury
Cover   [Front, Back]
Flyleaf   [i, 95, 96]

Artwork: Haiga Adventure Study Group
   of Puget Sound Sumi Artists

Melinda Brottem   [91, 92]
  "October Moon"   Haiga Collage

Darlene Dihel   [1, 2, 35]
  "Harvest Moon"   Sumi-e Haiga
  "Autumn Leaves"   Sumi-e Haiga

Judy Kalin   [83, 84]
  "Whispering Tree Tops"   Sumi Collage Haiga

Fumiko Kimura   [v, 53, 69, 81, 89]
  "Instant Haiku"   Fan Fold Haiga Book

Dorothy Matthews   [xv]
  "Spring"   Sumi-e Collage

Nora Shannon   [17, 71, 72]
  "Murderous Thoughts"   Haiga Collage

www.ingramcontent.com/pod-product-compliance
Lightning Source LLC
Chambersburg PA
CBHW071716040426
42446CB00011B/2085